Kaleidoscope
of
Colliding Hopes

Volume 1

Poems & Lyrics
by
Codey Cross

Dedicated to the so few memories
That don't make me feel sick...

...And to all of you
Who were a part of it

Harmony in Tragedy

Everything's going to be alright now
There is no need to cry now
Don't shed one more tear
The angels are buried below us
The demons may hover around us
But all they're going to hear is

You and me
In harmony
Singing such sweet melodies
Matching the beat in our hearts
And even if it kills me
You will be happy
Just you wait and see
Our new start

You're entombed deeper than the ocean blue
With photographs of a past that make you blue
So many highs and lows that make you twist
The evil in the world continues to burn
While the light in your life has been burnt out
You reminisce about all the times that you miss

You and me
In harmony
Singing such sweet melodies
Matching the beat in our hearts
And even if it kills me
You will be happy
Just you wait and see
Our new start

You ask me how a heart can break again and again
And I swear to you each time its because it mends
—
Their impact remains though they'll never awake
But if one lives forever in the light they make
Is this really the end of

You and me
In harmony
Singing such sweet melodies
Matching the beat in our hearts
And even if it kills me
You will be happy
Just you wait and see
Our new start
Just you wait and see
Our new start
Just you wait and see
Our new start

Farewell

You were the light of my life
The soul that kept me strong
And just as things were going right
Everything went wrong
Staring at you in your hospital bed
There's nothing I can do
I have lost a few too many
Don't tell me that I'm losing you

Kiss the ground goodbye
And through the clouds you'll fly
The only star in sight
Is the one you became tonight

Desperately, I've listened to
That song a thousand times
Going mad, excessively
Reading between the lines
Losing sleep looking for
What I know I'll never find
There is no rhyme or reason
Why you had to die

Kiss the ground goodbye
And through the clouds you'll fly
The only star in sight
Is the one you became tonight

So swallow your pills
Even though you're not ill
And I bet you're not happy still
But suddenly you're very still

So kiss the ground goodbye
And through the clouds you'll fly
The only star in sight
Is the one you became tonight
I'll close my eyes
To be with you in the sky
I'd give up my life
To see you one last time

I'll close my eyes
To be with you in the sky
I'd give up my life
To see you one last time

The Making Of

As someone numb to everything
I felt your touch
Not simply with spreading your lips, your legs
And such
Nor even our talks, our caresses
Your clutch
But rather all the encompassing in between
And the making of –

For someone who believes in nothing
I believed in us
Not that we'd be forever
But at least in our love
Our time may come and go
But let's carry all the hope, the trust
And all the chaos and clarity we've created
And the making of –
The making of love
The making of us

Without Me

Everything's the same
Save an insignificant difference
A trivial vacancy
Nothing necessarily missed

Some my argue
Things are a little better
The few I knew
May care if they remember
But most won't have a clue
No concern when I left or entered

Nothing I have built
Can't be done better now
If I'm worth sticking around
Please tell me how

I try to stay self-confident
Believe in the clichés
Live a life an idealist
Ill make it my own way
But I believe in the opposite
I won't be something some day

This is the world without me
This is the world without me
This is the world without me

And as you can see
Nothing's changed

A Couple Chords and a Whole Lot of Heart

A couple chords and a whole lot of heart
I knew you wouldn't stay from the very start
But I will try to have faith in us
Because I'm in love
Some sincere words I wrote with my whole heart
Try to sound smart then I'll hide it in the art
Because I know you'll tear it apart
But I don't know what it is you want
But I'll pray every day that
You want us

If this song doesn't work out
I'll just have to write another
Knowing if I asked you
You'd say to never bother
But darling, its never been a bother
In fact its always been my honor
And if our lives don't work out
We'll always have each other
You know I need you
But you could do much better
But doll, you make me better
Because you make me happier
And I'll pray everyday
You'll be my lover

I love you
Do you love me too
You swore to me
That you do indeed
Then you kissed me on my cheek
And fulfilled all my dreams
But then my heart began to sink
When it wasn't as it seemed
Told me it was past feelings
That shouldn't have come back up
But like I said in the beginning
I'll always have faith in us
Because I'm in love

Perpetual Progress

A product of my past
Is thinking far too narrow
And the choices I make today
Do not define who I am tomorrow
My mind is not set in stone
Nor in bone down to the marrow

Learn to Listen

I find
If we all could just sit in silence
Seize a moment and learn to listen
We would find there's no victory in violence
Otherwise
Your voice carries in false volition
Keeping loud and proud in ignorance
Be weary the weakness of words without this lesson

Those Ghosts

Your spirit is just like the moon
One side dances along with this tune
While the other hides in black facing doom
Safe to say we'll all meet that side soon

It seems to me your giving up on everything
And we can't do anything
You're drifting deeper into space
But I'll always be here waiting

When we look up at the stars
The light that shines is from a far
Distant past light years from where we are
Living the end, we only we the start

Maybe that's how it works for me and you
Visions in my head swear it's true
The sight of you still remains
With only memories to hold on to

Surrounded by the ghosts
That I love the most
I swear they'd follow me
From coast to coast
It's hard to tell how I feel
About this whole deal
But I'm starting to need
Those ghosts

They say light never fades away
So promise me you will always stay
Expanding farther until one day
The whole universe can see your face

Everyday I feel like such a mess
Seeing ghosts, am I cursed or blessed
Can't tell if I'm going insane
So I'll just keep trying to make sense
Of it all

Surrounded by the ghosts
That I love the most
I swear they'd follow me
From coast to coast
It's hard to tell how I feel
About this whole deal
But I'm starting to need
Those ghosts
Those ghosts

Heroin's the Best

Awake
My mind begins to take
Asleep
You'd think I'd have a break
But alas
My head begins to ache
Awake
Fall asleep for heaven's sake

Sour insomnia
You won't get the best out of me
I'll leave you soon
And I won't miss you
Because I want to be free
I want to believe
But I can't seem to see
What is right in front of me

Bitter and cold
I'm losing control
Can't seem to remember
All I've been told
Just take the drugs
And it'll do the rest
Pot, pills or booze
Heroin's the best

Maybe
They were on to something
Definitely
They were on something
I always thought
It was worse than anything
But maybe
Its better than nothing

Unwelcomed death
You aren't worth my breath
I have never even tried
A cigarette
But I want to be free
I want to believe
But I can't seem to see
What is right in front of me

Bitter and cold
I'm losing control
Can't seem to remember
All I've been told
Just take the drugs
And it'll do the rest
Pot, pills or booze
Heroin's the best

Porcelain Getaway

So whisper something in my ear
Something short and sweet my dear
And take me away
To much better days
I understand you loud and clear
Although I'm someone you hold near
I'm afraid
We're going separate ways

And I don't know what I want
But I think I'm ready for change
I'm ready for anything at all
And I
Got some things to work out

Like I know you are not mine
But thank you anyway
Just to have you on my mind
Is enough to make me stay
My porcelain getaway

In my head we're making love
Long conversations and such
And I know its strange
To think this way
But with you all I'm thinking of
Is just how breathtaking you are
And I'm dreaming all day
You'll see my way

And I now know what I want
And that's for you to be happy
Even if that doesn't include me
But I
Can't live without

I know you are not mine
But I'm yours either way
Thank you for your time
I treasure all our days
You were always so kind
Taught me love was okay
To share with all I find
But I still need to say
You'll always hold a special place
My porcelain getaway

Late Night or Early Morning?

Candle's burnt at both ends with the midnight oil
Profound or pretentious, a mind's night of toil
Pondering far past the point of enlightened, now turmoil
Poetic or pathetic, I tread on existential soil

My conscience holds a universe, my body a temple
In my eyes it's clear, you can see them resemble
All of space and time broken down and disassembled
So deep, dark, and vast just the thought makes me tremble

And each one of us carries such a profound nature
All together creating a single being of strangers
A collective consciousness of something greater
Connected to the earth, moon, stars and each other

I find if we are all just one entangled mess of threads
Tied to one another by the chaos in our heads
Our knots should not leave me so alone, instead
I should be with all of you, I feel I've been mislead

There's just me, my mind, and a single cigarette
Getting lost in thought encased in stars and my own breathe
Digging myself deeper inside an emotional cassette
Experiencing life alone hoping this isn't as good as it gets

I'm Half Way There

You have to fail fantastically
In order to succeed spectacularly

Rockin' All the Time

I'm bitter like my coffee
You're my something sweet
Keeps my heart beating
Our favorite song on repeat
I'm already off rhythm
You're always swinging to the beat
So why don't we dance together
Do some magic with our feet

If baby I'm a jukebox
Doll you're a dime
Why don't you say we get together
Keep it rockin' all the time
I know that I'm a mess
But you're always so fine
Complete chaos with each other
We'd keep it rockin' all the time

We share all our blues
Thrived off of punk and rock 'n' roll
And while I was screaming my heart out
You sang with all your soul
And of course I'm out of key
But you never said a word
Just cried along with me
Much louder than the radio

If baby I'm a jukebox
Doll you're a dime
Why don't you say we get together
Keep it rockin' all the time
I know that I'm a mess
But you're always so fine
Complete chaos with each other
We'd keep it rockin' all the time

And I get so bored
Lordy lord
I get so bored
But with you
Belle of the ball
I have been cured
Nothing else interests me
As genuinely and pure
As you my darling
You're all that I live for

If baby I'm a jukebox
Doll you're a dime
Why don't you say we get together
Keep it rockin' all the time
I know that I'm a mess
But you're always so fine
Complete chaos with each other
We'd keep it rockin' all the time

In My Head

Buried in my bed
Minds distant, I'm dead
Its too late
Can't take back
The things that I've said

Beneath the blood shed
Is crimson condemned
I've gave in
Forgive me
I won't kill again

I don't make my own choices
It's up to the voices
I don't make my own choices
It's up to the voices
I don't make my own choices
It's up to the voices
In my head

Sanity is spread
Hanging by a thread
I'm trying
But losing
On thin ice I tread

By being I've bled
I risk being misread
To leave
Or live
Intact but instead

I don't make my own choices
It's up to the voices
I don't make my own choices
It's up to the voices
I don't make my own choices
It's up to the voices
In my head

Homesick

So many
People love me
But I'm still lonely
I'm so sorry
I'm trying
To make you proud of me
But I'm not happy
And I hate this city

I'm homesick
I'm homesick
And I don't need this
I'm going home
Again

I don't need your stuff
No I don't need much
Just give me your love
Yes, that's more than enough
Fighting back fears
That failure is near
And time has made it clear
I fucking hate it here

I'm homesick
I'm homesick
And I don't need this shit
I'm going home
Again

It Was a Work Night

Morning be damned
For love is a duel!

An Open Letter

I want a soul as sturdy as oak
Feet rooted deep down in the ground
I'm never coming out
Soul so heavy
Like a glorious anchor
Shaped as antlers
Branching out towards each and everyone
Dragged so down I'm barnacle bound

I have a heart that's as hard as stone
So thick its even held its own
Blow after blow
Heart big but cold
As a glacier still solid
Like my hands so callused
Reaching out for anyone
I'm so fucked though, I let everyone go

And there's a mighty hole
Gaping through my fragile soul
The kind that makes an
Otherwise decent man broke and bent
But thanks to you
I feel whole
Again

I want a soul that flows with the space
Minds drifting, freely floating away
It's never out of place
Soul so light
Like a hot air balloon
As big as the moon
Large enough to hold each and everyone
You light my flame and I'll hold all of your pain

I have a heart that's as dull as dirt
So flexible, fluid, and used
After years of abuse
Heart's still full but hurt
Pretty pathetic
Yet so empathetic
I have compassion for anyone
From the beaten and bruised, to all those accused

And there's a mighty hole
Gaping through my fragile soul
The kind that makes an
Otherwise decent man broke and bent
But thanks to you
I know my role
Thanks to you
I'm in control
Yes, thanks to you
I feel whole
Again

Hypocritical Dick

I'm an apple that fell
To far from the tree
Through my father's eyes
I am the bad seed
I'm too hard to love,
Because I'm so different
Getting by an outcast
I'm simply trying to live

I'm not a freak
I'm just unique
Somebody out there
Has to know what I mean
I try to love
Now I'm desperate
Such a dick
I'm a hypocrite

Stomping on weeds
Only make them strive
Ivy must move up
So like the vines, I will try to climb
I'm not a Camilla
Rather, just indecisive
And whenever I open my mouth
Your words get so abusive

But I was a match
And when you struck me
It only lit a flame
Igniting me
Now I try to love
So desperate
Such a dick
I'm a hypocrite

So hateful
But full of love
I never lie
You caught my bluff
You hate me
Well I make me sick
Narcissistic
A hypocritical dick

Saints, Sinners, and Such

I won't judge you
For selling yourself
Whether at a corner or church
I can't say what's better or worse

My Future at Best

Mind of wine
Better with age
But body of vinegar
Bitter to taste

Our Fire

You're beginning to look homely
Leaves are falling slowly
Starting to feel lonely
Though you're loved by many
You're afraid
But fight bravely

Watch all your favorite colors
Your mother and your father
All your past lovers
Everything has changed
But we'll always
Have each other

So take everything you have
And everything you've learned
Throw it in a fire and let it all burn
It's time to start over
It's time to take a turn
For better or for worse
Throw it in a fire and let it all burn

As summer shifts to fall
And you start to lose it all
Just give me a call
And I'll remind you again
You've always
Loved the fall

It's been a time of love
And sometimes it's been tough
But when you've had enough
You know I'll be there
To catch you
When things get rough

So take everything you have
And everything you've learned
Throw it in a fire and let it all burn
It's time to start over
It's time to take a turn
For better or for worse
Throw it in a fire and let it all burn

I know things aren't the way they use to be
Please try to close your eyes and count to three
You'll find yourself lying down next to me
By this fire we built together under this tree
And you'll start to finally see
Things haven't changed, were just growing

So take everything you have
And everything you've learned
Throw it in a fire and let it all burn
It's time to start over
It's time to take a turn
For better or for worse
Throw it in a fire and let it all burn

Another Sip, Another Sigh

Another sip, another sigh
Working another nine to five
I've come to dread this life
Living paycheck to paycheck
Starting to feel like a wreck
What I'd give just for some rest
But that's not the life I live
Tonight's another shift
There's no time to be a kid
I'm begging something's got to give
There's more to life than this
Yes, it comes in a cup full of bliss

Sitting back with my cup of coffee
By the patio with a view of the world
They never seem to glance back at me
But at least the scene is beautiful

Another sip, another sigh
The shit that's running through my mind
Is enough to make a grown man cry
Doing such mindless work
Conscience fucks me like a whore
I want to be something more
Existential thoughts make
All my neurons fire away
Like a gun going off in my brain
I'm tired of being fake
Tired of waiting for something great
I'm begging whistle blow for break
Before I break

Sitting back with my cup of coffee
by the patio with a view of the world
It never seems to glance back at me
But at least the scene is beautiful
Thinking about everything and nothing
Sun warms my cheek but my drink is cold
Now that I've finished my cup of coffee
Its time to go back into the world

RockaBye

So rockabye me baby
Before you leave
Put me to sleep
Put me out of my misery

I know you plan to go
Never expected you to stay
No one ever does
But I'm never quite prepared
To lose those I do
When the day comes

So rockabye me baby
So maybe, just maybe
I'll rest in peace
Dying while it's still
You and me

Key Words are Could Have

She's an old soul
Genuine and vintage
Plays me easy like piano keys
A semi-melancholy image
As the world carried us on her shoulders
We could have built an empire
Molded entirely out of
Dreams, dust, and our desire

Midst of an Apocalypse

The countdown starts
But they'll stop it at one
Just to build the suspension
Anticipation
Then the world tears apart
As the sky rains its bombs
Just to get our attention
Obliteration

For all the land
There is nothing left worth holding
Men and women with a lack of hope
Comatose
Blistered feet with filthy hands
What's there to say for the children
Boys and girls with a lack of home
Overdose

We're in the midst
Of an apocalypse
As twisted as it seems
You won't want to miss

The boiling seas
The toxic breeze
The burning trees
And bloody screams
Your final squeeze
You cling to me
It's time to see
Eternity
'Cause we won't die
Its not our time
Our bodies lie
But we still fly
Through the midst
Of an apocalypse
I sense peace
Beyond all this

The debris settles
Whats left is unfathomable
Sparks living with night internal
Nocturnal
The end of battles
A place that remains beautiful
Regardless of anyone seeing it external
Eternal

I Want to be Free

There's a world out there to see
With seven lands and seven seas
And a whole lot of ocean in between
I want to be free
I'm going to climb every mountain I see
From the lowest of valleys
To the highest of peaks
And I'm going to do it all just for me
I want to be free

Free from the torment of sin
And all the poor places that I've been
Escape this mess
The hell, the debt
I'm so depressed
With life and death
Someone please hear my plea
I want to be free

There's a whole multi-verse to see
With all these planes and galaxies
There are so many possibilities
I want to be free
I'm going to explore all of me
From every flaw
To each bit of hope I foresee
Find a balance in madness like space debris
I want to be free

Tell me where do I begin
Scarred my skin, my faith's gone thin
Nonetheless
I've undressed and confessed
Tore my heart
outside my chest
Stretching out with the trees
I want to be free

All I Need

All I need's my guitar
My harmonica
And a pack of cards
As for the rest
You can have it
Yes, you can have it all
But my love
Because that belongs to all

All you need in life
Is just a little soul
A whole lot of love
Old-fashioned rock and roll
And freedom is the last of it
Well maybe a lady to share it with
That's all you need in life
And not a whole lot more

I'm telling you
Money isn't real
Though you may disagree
That's just how I feel
And I'll always take
Experience over materials
And ownership
Well thats the devil's deal

All you need in life
Is just a little soul
A whole lot of love
Old-fashioned rock and roll
And freedom is the last of it
Well maybe a lady to share it with
That's all you need in life
And not a whole lot more

Aftertaste

You're the burn in my lungs
In each cigarette
You're what's on my mind
When it comes to regrets
You're what I can't seem to forgive
Let alone forget

To Be Brave

With all these fears
I'm no longer afraid
While they leave me
Anxious and scared
They also give me the chance
To be brave

By Storm

She's a mess at the moment
Not quite jaded, but tired
Rings surrounding her eyes
But they're filled with a fire
Determined with dreams
Desires reaching much higher
A girl with goals
Ready for tomorrow

Watching her at her worst
Is still something to admire
She takes her own pace
Struggles only inspire
Her and those all around
As she ambitiously aspires
Mirroring her eyes with
That passionate glow

She never complains
When it rains
Rides the tides
And rolls with the waves
In a flash of thunder
Watch her transform
She's taking the world by storm

She's so sorry for who she is
Unaware of her empire
Says she'll be something someday
Shines best when it's down to the wire
Don't you already know
You're preaching to the choir
I say tell me something
I don't already know

She never complains
When it rains
Rides the tides
And rolls with the waves
In a flash of thunder
Watch her transform
She's taking the world by storm

We all wane
As we wade
Through the shores
Of better days
Whereas you seem to
Rise with the wake
Yet promises to be so much more
She's taking the world by storm

Write for Your Life

I write and I write
All day and all night
Though try as I might
With ink or graphite
Onto white
I still wonder
Where is the light
What is right

Midwest Weather

If your mind changes
As often as the color in your hair
Then by tomorrow
I doubt I'll be here
If your taste is as fickle
As the Midwest weather
Then I find it hard to believe
Anything for you
Can mean forever

More Than Memories

Wake me in the morning
Say you'll never leave
Wake me in the morning
Swear you still love me
Last night was special
We prayed it'd never end
But seeing you this morning
I look forward to the weekend

Because I love our memories
But I love you now
And before to long
We'll be sharing our vows

Wake me in the morning
Sing me a song
Wake me in the morning
We've slept in to long
I never want to leave
Lets stay in bed today
Get up ASAP
I'm looking forward to our day

Because I love our memories
But I love you now
And before to long
We'll be sharing our vows
To relive those moments
All I'd have to do
Is hold your hand tight
And fall again for you
For you

Wake me in the morning
So I can fall again for you

Hope is a Choice

Even a bird with a broken wing
Will still find it in her heart to sing
So what will you do
It's up to you
Even a man who has nothing
Will still find the joy in everything
Whatever path you choose
I'll stay with you

Vanity

She sits at her vanity in vain
Starring into the mirror

When did I begin to wane
Where did I find this fear

Peace, Love, and Anarchy

Tonight's the night I'll end this fight
Swallow these words, spit out my pride
I don't know why things aren't alight
But no more swords, there are just two sides

One half's hate, the other's peace
Yin and yang, no in between
Live for love and anarchy
Challenge change, hear my plea
And push for peace

Take my soul for what its worth
My life's soil, its all just dirt
Its not a lot and its going to hurt
But I'll give everything I've got for a better Earth

Don't fight back, nor run or hide
To raise your fist is to join their side
In the end peace will rise
Or all of us are going to die
With hate's demise

I find this world so beautiful
So much compassion for all its people
But something wrong, its all fucked up
Every war hurts all of us
Money gained, lives lost
All these gods, all our trust
We live our lives a constant fight
No end but ours are in sight

Kill for a cause but at what cost
Any war fought is another lost
Anarchy, love, and peace
A symphony of you and me
And if I die, that's quite alright
I'd live my life for what I felt was right
I'm on my knees, I'm begging please
It's all our end, or harmony
I'll die for peace
I'll die for peace

To Hell With the Ungrateful

If there is a God
I'm not asking to be forgiven
To go to Hell
Making me appreciate all that I had
Sounds like my kind of heaven

Where I Longed to Enter, You Saw an Exit

When one door closes
Another two open
But the path you shut behind you
Blocked off with locks broken
Is the only way I wish to go
At least I was hoping

Color Me Serenity

So color me
Serenity
A false sense of hope
Fill me in
Brightly
And never let go

So color me
Serenity
Flood my foolish mind
Mercifully
With amenity
If you would be so kind

So color me
Serenity
Variegate my veins
Obscured identity
In obscenity
Be weary as I wane

So color me
Serenity
Falsify my fantasies
Shade in the
Insanities
Exaggerate my affinities

Wishful Thinking

Why must the brightest
Always burn out first
Leaves us all
When we need them the most
Deserving of chariots
Leaves in a hearse
You're so far away
Yet feel so close
At least I tell myself

Vacant Hearts

Vacant hearts
Once so valiant
Now violently torn apart
Forever absent

Formerly an open sea
While vast and free
Was susceptible and naïve
Forthwith familiar to vulnerability

Affection and benevolence
Was flooded with betrayal and departure
Our ocean void became desolate
Perspective shifts like tide to the shore

Emotions, though abundantly deep, have gave
As we are too afraid to be saved
Remember us as we used to be, compassionate and brave
As today, such warmth comes and goes in waves

Platonic Affair

Every now and again
You amaze me
Atonement of my sins
You break me
Everything you've been
Has sustained me
But I'm not the only one

I'm Allergic Anyway

She took a chance
Plucked each daisy
Picked each petal
Yes, no, maybe
Letting flowers
Choose destiny
Are we in love
Or history
Well by the end
My luck would be
She loves me not
Fuck flowers

Which is Worse

More focused on
Drugs and ego
Quite frankly
About to overdose on both

100

— In a flash she was there
Bright and bold, the embodiment of desire
Began as a simple flame, but now a mighty fire
She was my guide against the dark
Burning bright with me as a spark
As I was delicate and cold
She provided me warmth in her hold
My heart once hollow as a dreary, deflated balloon
She was the blaze that lifted me to the moon
I was once fading away
Now could never live without
I longed for her light but got too close and burned
And just like that, she burned out

Sleep or Lack There of

Self-loathing melancholy
Cut too deep
Within the veins of insomnia
I must've murdered sleep

Sibylline

I need you
So sibylline
Wise and aware
To hold on to me
And lie
Like you care
Make prophesies
Everything's fine
I'll make you swear
Break these promises
After I die
Sorry life's not fair
But do this for me
This one time
I'm so scared
Do this for me
One last time

Bucket List

Don't die

The Idea of Me

I'll take back
Another cigarette
Breath in the cancer
And out the regrets
I've got nothing to live for
Nothing at all
Living in a world so small

I watch as the smoke
Dissipates above my head
Searing at the other end
Another ember turns red
One fades away
While the other burns out
I wonder which way is my route

Give me anything to fall asleep
Then something to stay awake
I've done everything I could
Though I know I've been given more than I gave
So let me carry myself to my grave

When I was young
Slightly more innocent and high strung
I probably stood a chance
But now I'm long gone
I'm much too tired and hung up
On what's in my head
More or less among the dead

I spend all day taking things to stay awake
So much coffee and meds, there's no telling my intake
When the moon rolls up
I do all I can to fall asleep
Everything I can but weep

I would if I could and heaven knows I've tried
There seems to be something wrong with my eyes
Time's taken all their color and life
It appears I've become dry

I'm sorry I'm not as strong as you think
Sorry I'll never be the potential you see
The longer I stay, the more diluted I become
Polluting the image that everyone saw
But if I die now, survives the possibility
You'll all treasure what could've been and fond memories
Though I never felt pressured, please believe
But I could never live up to the idea of me

I guess, I guess, yes I guess I did my best
And although it wasn't good enough
Haven't I earned some rest
This life beat the living shit out of me
Do I not at least deserve death

No? so
I'll take back another cigarette
Breath in the cancer and out the regrets
Pretend I've got so much to live for
As far as you know
Living in such a large world

Here I Hang

So here I hang
But the noose is loose
No cord could hold me
And my truth
So there I lay
But with no time to lose
I have too many to live for
And far to much to do

And I will find my own escape
But unlike you
I will live to see another day
There'll be no noose
Nor chemicals to my brain
And I alone
Will determine my own fate
So here I hang
So here I hang

So here I hang
But its not on a rope
I dangle
From the thin threads of hope
So there I stay
And I'm trying to cope
But not with the drugs that you chose
Nor the cables where you choked

And I will find my own escape
But unlike you
I will live to see another day
There'll be no noose
Nor chemicals to my brain
And I alone
Will determine my own fate
So here I hang
So here I hang

So here I hang
So here I hang
So here I hang
So here I hang
So here I hang
So here I —

Wake Me Up

Wake me up
I've been asleep
You've been able to keep
Me
From falling
Off my own two feet

Lift me up
But break me down
I've been breaking down
Now
I'll do my best
Not to make a sound

You are my rock
You are my soul
And by the time I'm gray and old
I need you to know
By our fading locks
And your heart of gold
You're my silver lining
When I need it the most

Let me in
Free feelings in stride
With nothing to hide
Lie
Down, with these words
By your bedside

Breathe me in
So spirits coincide
Our hearts collide
And I
Melt into you
As we confide

You are my rock
You are my soul
Before to long I'll be gone so
I need to know
You'll always be
All you promised to me
All I know you too be
And you'll move on happy

You are my rock
You are my soul
And before I'm nothing more than I ghost
I need you to know
If I should die
Before I wake
There'll be no need to pray
I'm all yours to take
But please –

Wake me up

Just a Thought

Without a judge
There are no sinners
No right or wrong
Losers or winners
We live content
Like life was meant
To be
We were meant to be
Free

I've been through a lot
Seen some shit along the way
No one knows the things I've fought
But along my walks
I found reasons to be happy today
I don't know
It was just a thought

Is it so hard to love
So hard not to give up
I guess so
But what do I know
If we gave up
What we had
And took in
All their laughs
Then well, who knows
I know I don't

I've been through a lot
Seen some shit along the way
No one knows the things I've fought
But along my walks
I found reasons to be happy today
I don't know
It was just a thought

And as swift as it came
It was gone —

STRAY CAT STUDIOS